Level 1.7
Points 0.5

MONSTER
Tractors

by Chris Bowman

BELLWETHER MEDIA • MINNEAPOLIS, MN

Note to Librarians, Teachers, and Parents:

Blastoff! Readers are carefully developed by literacy experts and combine standards-based content with developmentally appropriate text.

Level 1 provides the most support through repetition of high-frequency words, light text, predictable sentence patterns, and strong visual support.

Level 2 offers early readers a bit more challenge through varied simple sentences, increased text load, and less repetition of high-frequency words.

Level 3 advances early-fluent readers toward fluency through increased text and concept load, less reliance on visuals, longer sentences, and more literary language.

Level 4 builds reading stamina by providing more text per page, increased use of punctuation, greater variation in sentence patterns, and increasingly challenging vocabulary.

Level 5 encourages children to move from "learning to read" to "reading to learn" by providing even more text, varied writing styles, and less familiar topics.

Whichever book is right for your reader, Blastoff! Readers are the perfect books to build confidence and encourage a love of reading that will last a lifetime!

This edition first published in 2014 by Bellwether Media, Inc.

No part of this publication may be reproduced in whole or in part without written permission of the publisher. For information regarding permission, write to Bellwether Media, Inc., Attention: Permissions Department, 5357 Penn Avenue South, Minneapolis, MN 55419.

Library of Congress Cataloging-in-Publication Data

Bowman, Chris, 1990-
  Monster Tractors / by Chris Bowman.
      pages cm – (Blastoff! Readers. Monster Machines)
  Includes bibliographical references and index.
  Audience: Age 5-8.
  Audience: Grades K to 3.
  Summary: "Developed by literacy experts for students in kindergarten through grade three, this book introduces tractors to young readers through leveled text and related photos"– Provided by publisher.
  ISBN 978-1-62617-055-1 (hardcover : alk. paper)
  1. Tractors–Juvenile literature. 2. Monster trucks–Juvenile literature. I. Title.
  TL233.15.B69 2014
  631.3'72–dc23
                              2013035105

Table of Contents
Contents

Monster Tractors!

Farmers use big tractors to **plow** fields.

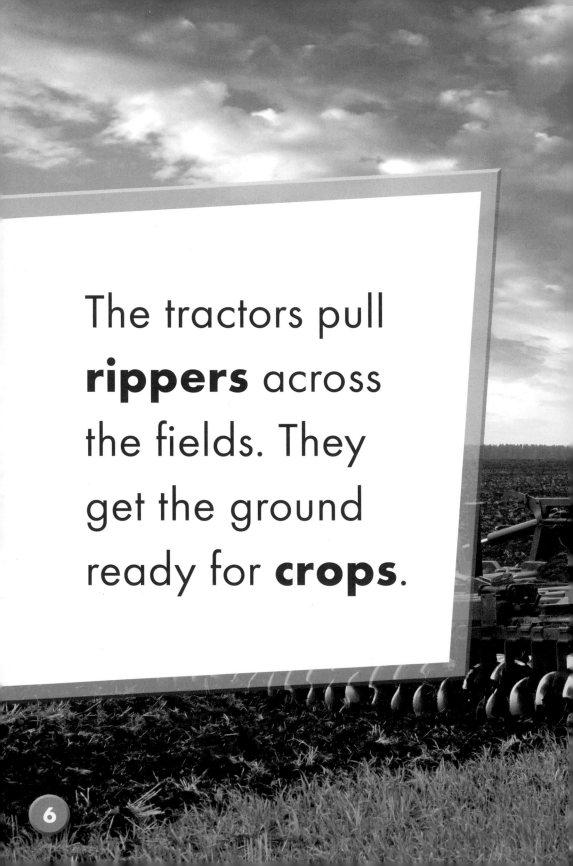

The tractors pull **rippers** across the fields. They get the ground ready for **crops**.

ripper

Tractors also pull **spreaders**. These tools spread seeds and **fertilizer**.

spreader

Parts That Pull

Farm tractors have big **engines**. They need a lot of power even at slow speeds.

engine

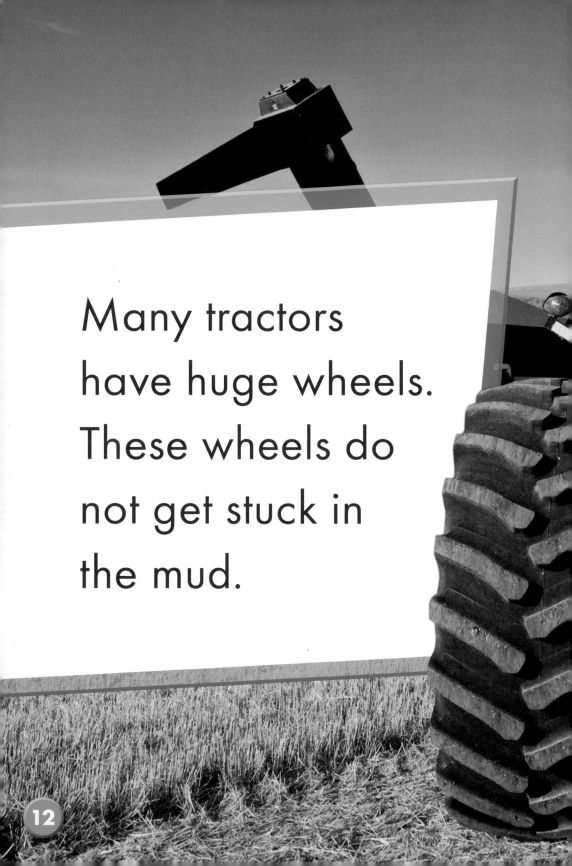

Many tractors have huge wheels. These wheels do not get stuck in the mud.

Others have **tracks**. These tractors move well on bumpy ground.

tracks

Tractor Pulls

The strongest tractors compete in **tractor pulls**.

16

Tractor pulling is called the most powerful **motorsport**.

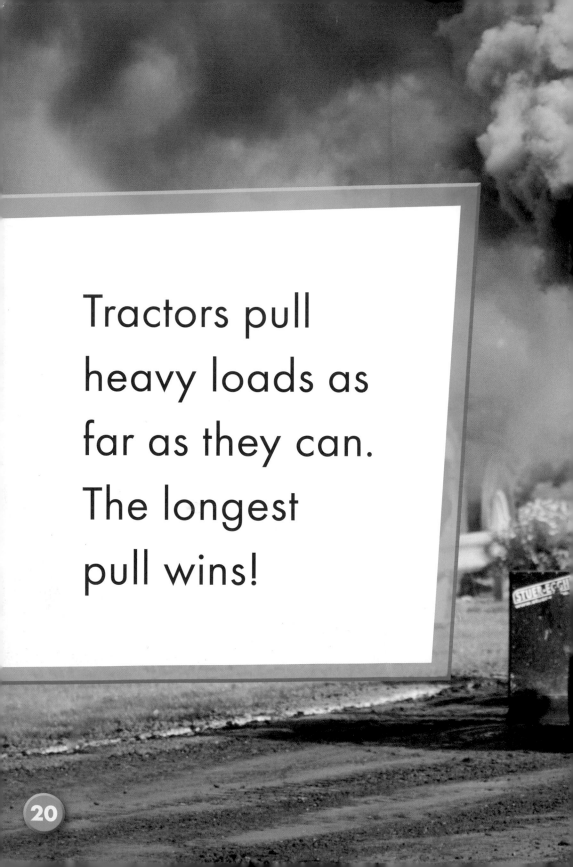

Tractors pull
heavy loads as
far as they can.
The longest
pull wins!

Glossary

crops—plants grown for food

engines—machines that power vehicles

fertilizer—something that makes soil better for growing crops

motorsport—a sport that involves vehicles powered by engines

plow—to break up and turn ground

rippers—tools that break up the ground

spreaders—tools that spread seeds and fertilizer across fields

tracks—large belts that move over a series of wheels

tractor pulls—competitions where tractors pull heavy loads a long distance

To Learn More

AT THE LIBRARY

Alexander, Heather. *Big Book of Tractors.*
New York, N.Y.: Parachute Press, 2007.

Coppendale, Jean. *Tractors and Farm
Vehicles*. Richmond Hill, Ont.: Firefly Books,
2010.

Nichols, Catherine. *Tractor Power!* New York,
N.Y.: DK Publishing, 2009.

ON THE WEB

Learning more about
tractors is as easy as 1, 2, 3.

1. Go to www.factsurfer.com.

2. Enter "tractors" into the search box.

3. Click the "Surf" button and you will see a
   list of related Web sites.

With factsurfer.com, finding more information
is just a click away.

Index

The images in this book are reproduced through the courtesy of: SimplyCreativePhotography, front cover; tanger, pp. 4-5; Vladimir Salman, pp. 6-7; FLPA/ SuperStock, pp. 8-9; Taina Sohlman, pp. 10-11; Raimund Kutter Image Broker/ Newscom, p. 11 (small); AgStock Images, Inc./ Alamy, pp. 12-13; Rick Dalton/ Alamy, pp. 14-15; Egon Bomsch/ East Liverpool Review/ Associated Press, pp. 18-19; PicturesByRob/ Alamy, pp. 20-21.